The Art of Being a Soccer Agent

Keys to excelling in a fascinating profession

Paúl Fraga

To my father

To Emilie

To my mother wherever she is

Table of Contents

I

II

PART I UNDERSTANDING THE PROFESSION OF A SOCCER AGENT

1. INTRODUCTION

I don't know you, but in my case every time I look for literature regarding soccer players' agents, always happens the same. The only thing I find is a lot of books, pretty thick (I must say), with the things to do, step by step, to become a soccer agent. Nothing else. Just that. They seem textbooks. They are a series of objective data and general rules you need to know and learn but that don't go beyond that. They are neutral, helpless. They don't take side.

It's like law. One thing is to learn law and quite another to practice law. As José Hermida, (friend and communication expert) would say "they are books that give you a tin can but, however, don't give you the opener to open it." And because of that, with this book, I want to be your opener.

This is the book that I would have liked to read when I started in this profession. Wouldn't you like someone that apart from telling you WHAT the profession is about tells you as well HOW to practice it? If so, this is your book.

Can you imagine how would you feel if you could know what you'll find in this activity? If you could know how to avoid mistakes? How would you feel if you could find out what are the key things of the profession and you could have the right tools?

You can find the answers to your questions in the following pages. I had to suffer it in my own skin to explain it to you now. I will tell you how to take advantage of important issues and avoid mistakes I made and that I don't want you to make. Are you ready? Here we go!

Let me start by telling you that I am passionate about my profession. I find it really comforting. If the possibility of playing this profession has crossed your mind, I invite you to give a step forward, to be brave and to be committed with your desire. But you must be really committed, because you'll need commitment in abundance. And that can be generated and self-imposed, not bought.

Everyone talks about the benefits and sex-appeal about being a soccer agent. And all the glamor it generates. I won't tell whether it has it or not. For me that's indifferent. What really concerns me, and what I want to convey, is that everything is not glitter. Nothing further from the truth. I don't want to be discouraging. I'll explain myself.

Being a soccer agent could resemble a duck, calm on the surface, tireless work underwater. This is a very nice, different, special, sui generis activity, but we also talk about an activity idealized by some, while vilified by others. Who hasn't heard occasionally "agents are thieves who care only for themselves"? I have heard that many times and I'm sure that you as well. It is true that there are some that behave like that but no more than what you can find in any other profession.

Being an agent is a vocation that has passion as fuel. The path is confusing, full of obstacles and troubles. And that's where you commitment should appear. Without it, forget it, you'll abandon. I've seen it many times. Or even worse, you'll simplify yourself" in the practice of the profession and you will be a short-term victim. Everything as a result of impatience and despair. But that is another story and I will talk about it later.

At this point I'll make mine a Friedrich Nietzsche expression: "if you know the why you can live any how". True. With a clear objective, opportunities arise by spontaneous generation. Now, if you want to pick the "fruit" without paying the price you will fall into despair at the slightest complexity. You have to enjoy the journey. In my case, for questions which interest me, I really pay the price willingly. Although I recognize that took me time.

When I decided to write this book I didn't want to be pretentious. Not at all. I rather wanted to give a series of strokes so people who read this book could have an idea of what is a soccer agent from a practical point of view. Also to make things more clear for people like you and show how does it work, its requirements and peculiarities, and what is most important to me, I wanted to give my particular vision of what for me is a good soccer agent. Obviously it is not an absolute truth, but it is my truth, personal and non-transferrable. If you continue until the end of the book you'll have the chance to know if you share my vision or not.

Throughout the book I will make a tour on the various issues to be addressed by an agent, and the way that, in my opinion, he should do it. We will talk about versatility, specialization, training, composure, mental strength, even languages. And, of course, management. In all its aspects.

Whatever, I hope that what follows is interesting and profitable for you. It took me time to realize many things and I want you to jump directly to the fast track.

2. <u>WHAT DOES A SOCCER AGENT DO?</u>

Quite often the same happens to me. Every time I go out for lunch or to have dinner with friends, or even in a family lunch, every time they ask me what I do and I tell them I'm a soccer agent the first thing they tell me is: "that's cool!!", and then they always make me the same question: "but a soccer agent, what really does? That's the million dollar question. I have never understood that. They say that they find being an agent amazing when they don't even have an idea of what it is. It is the ideal profession for holidays and birthdays. This episode occurs to me frequently and I don't think I'm the only one to whom that happens.

I'll tell you that a soccer agent helps his client (player or club) on everything he may need or request by charging a fee for it.

However, you may be wondering in what does the agent help and how he charges the fee for it. At this point we should make a distinction between the official and the unofficial.

The official states that an agent negotiates contracts on behalf of a player earning a percentage of the gross contract negotiated. It is also true that a player agent can also work for a particular club through a given mandate. In this case it will be the club itself that will determine the remuneration to be paid for the services rendered.

If you have a relative which is an habitual sports media reader and is not satisfied with the official explanation (they almost never do) you can always say that according to unofficial, the variables are a lot and diverse, and depend on each case (transfer percentage and advertising contracts, etc..). Perhaps this way he will be satisfied. In my case, by this time, I have not succeeded. I hope you have better luck.

Let's go on. Usually the agent signs a representation agreement, in exclusivity or not, with the player for a maximum duration of two years (top official). It is the player himself who is officially obliged to pay his agent directly for the agreed percentage (usually 10%). I insist on the word "official" because, for example, for this particular case, usually is the employer club that pays the agent directly. Apart from other issues, this is usually given to avoid the player get into tax issues.

That is, imagine that you have a signed agreement with your client so, in return for your services, the player will reward you with 10% of the gross contract negotiated. If the official is fulfilled, you as an agent should pass a bill to your client for the amount involving 10%, but to this we would have to add VAT. Therefore, your client, as an individual and ultimate beneficiary of the services provided, should bear the tax rate without any possibility to deduct such VAT. This way, therefore, the player pays much more than what was agreed.

It is also true that generally, at certain levels, players have their own companies to, among other things, manage their image rights, so in these cases, what I mentioned would not happen. However, keep in mind what I've explained earlier to simplify things.

Therefore, to not adversely affect the interests of the player, the agent tends to agree with the employer club so is the club who is going to pay the remuneration of the agent by express mandate of the player. Thus, the employer considers the amount received by the agent as part of the total wage of the player. So, consequently, tax issues such as VAT don't affect, as the club as a society can deduct the VAT.

At this point, I will make a distinction between what is a normal players' agent and what is commonly known as an intermediary. I have an opinion about it. It is true that players' agents often work as intermediaries, that is, acting as a liaison between what might be called supply and demand.

However, according to how I understand the profession, I wouldn't consider this performance as an issue that is properly part of the definition of agent. Let's say **there are many agents who also work as intermediaries, but not all intermediaries are agents**. In fact, when we talk about this profession we talk about an activity where many intruders prowl confused by the large figures that are used in the business. I hope you're not one of them.

Nor should we simplify the activity of players' agents as a mere team finder. It is clear that this is an important issue, however, despite being necessary, is not enough. Those who focus exclusively on this, neglecting other issues, are often people dazzled by quick profit, what is commonly called "have a hit". It is true that those exist, however, are nothing more than "noise" within the profession.

Partnerships between different agents that reach specific agreements to maximize the chances of success are also very common, bringing together the different capabilities of each of the agents.

There is another point to which we must pay special attention. At the time of this writing, being agent requires passing an examination that carry out the different national soccer associations. Officially, it is unavoidable to have this accreditation to perform the work.

However, regardless of the duly authorized agents, immediate family, as parents and siblings, are also allowed to perform this activity legally. However, it's not possible to place doors on an open field and ignore the preferences of who, after all, is the most important person: the soccer player.

Regardless of the barriers that can be put officially to carry out the activity, I think that little or nothing can be done if a player decides to put his trust in someone who lacks the required accreditation. It is like that. This profession is based on trust. Everything else is secondary. Even formalities.

Currently the possibility of a new regulation for the activity is being considered, giving another twist that may cause another jolt to the activity to which we have to adapt ourselves and get used to it. We'll see what happens.

3. __PROFESSION VS DEVOTION__

Ordinary mortals have absolutely idealized the soccer agent profession. People tend to see, through the media spotlight, only the final result that some obtain. Big names, big transfers, large numbers ultimately (That's why it's the perfect profession for holidays, birthdays and family lunches). And although you can find that, it is not the most common. To do a review of this profession by only emphasizing the final result is, apart from denoting a complete lack of knowledge, like thinking that appetizing red apples are made in series, in industrial lines.

I hope this is not your case, but if it is, sorry to disappoint you because if something seems to be an agent is precisely the opposite. It's the closest thing to craftsmanship you could ever meet. You must plant, water and let it grow. What you see is the tree, but most important is what you do not see: the roots.

Being a soccer players' agent is as closest thing to an obstacle race, but without regular wages along the path that makes things easier. Very often it is a faith act which is typical of the work in the shadow that is done for many months without the slightest glimmer of recognition about if you're doing right or wrong.

Specifically, __the recruitment of players is a simple attempt to capitalize a bet__. It's like the stock market. You see the stocks, you study past behaviors, you guess trends, you select one depending on countless variables, and you expect future behaviors.

And the stock/player can do two things: go up or down, hit or miss, success or failure. An absolutely studied and meditated bet but unpredictable. With a fundamental difference with the stock market. While in the stock market the opportunity to get a stock remains at a certain price set by supply and demand, in recruiting a player that variable does not exist. You get it or you don't. There is no a player breakdown. You can't get only his left leg, right hand and eyebrow. You know.

Moreover, definitely credibility and competition influence when you want to recruit a player. In the stock market, there is not such competition. There is one, of course. But there is one in a different way. In the stock market the large amounts competitors handle can selfishly vary the behavior of a stock. In soccer, when recruiting good players, those agents that have greater "pedigree" get the player. That's it. This issue is a great barrier to entry. Quite a challenge.

That's why it is not a usual profession. It has to dazzle you, you have to be fascinated about it. It has to be an absolute devotion. If not, you are lost. You'll abandon with the first hurdle. And as I explained, there are not obstacles, there are huge chasms that separate you from your objectives.

Without passion for this work it's impossible to overcome the problems, very difficult to stay focused on the objectives. You are absolutely convicted to love the way to go. That is like saying that one should enjoy the setbacks and frustrations. Well, yes. That is the case.

Be consistent. Success is not giving up, insist, trust your instinct, your abilities and your work. As Churchill said, *"Success consists on going from failure to failure without loss of enthusiasm"*. It's a job based on observation, instinct, know-how and, above all, credibility. Are you following me? Write this word down because perhaps it's the most important word in this book.

You might now ask yourself the following question: But how am I going to have credibility if any interesting to me soccer player gives me a chance to prove that I'm worthy of that credibility, and by extension, his confidence? Well, there you go the hieroglyphic. One should have the necessary self-confidence and tenacity to decrypt it.

However, that is not all. If you've just started and you've had the fortune and ability to recruit the player you were really interested in, usually at lower categories, you need to keep attentive because if your player stands out as a top player, he will likely arouse the attention of those agents with more credibility, notoriety, popularity, etc.., and will attempt to get your player. And, at least, your client will hear them. Don't fool yourself. It's like that. Hence the importance of providing value.

But there is always a first time and to get it you have to be tenacious, strong, intuitive, brave, insightful and essentially a great professional. Hence the need to be a true devotee of this activity. Because the beginning costs a lot. Although it is achieved with devotion and constancy. I assure you.

4. <u>AN APTITUDE AND ATTITUDE ISSUE</u>

Being a good agent is essentially a matter of attitude but also aptitude. As in other professions if today you want to be someone important in this particular world you have to be a great professional and be different. This is the capital mistake that many new agents make.

Very often many agents who decide to undertake this new adventure begin euphoric abducted by the connotations of this profession, and they really don't know the peculiarities and vicissitudes of the business. Being there is not enough. It is not enough to have a card. It is not enough the particular self-promotion campaigns that some do where you seem to be more than you are. That attitude won't take you too long.

It is only necessary to scrape a little bit to realize that everything is papier mache, like if it was a Disney set.

Thus, we must go further. You have to be very good at what you do.

a. <u>BECOME A LEONARDO DA VINCI</u>

"Those who fall in love with practice without theory are like pilots without rudder or compass, they will never be able to know where they're going". Leonardo Da Vinci.

These times consistently remind us the importance of specialization. That it is essential to be good at one thing. That to know about everything leads absolutely nowhere. Well. I do not buy that argument. At least not as far as being a soccer agent. We are rather talking about the opposite. Specialize yourself in the activity, not in knowledge! Attention, there is nothing wrong about knowing much about a particular thing, but you should know a little of everything, although later services are subcontracted.

You have to know about soccer, yes, but also about sales, finance, psychology, law, etc. And that's where a lot of new effusive agents fail. Or directly are not interested.

A good general and multidisciplinary education is absolutely essential to be a good agent. Otherwise, you're not an agent with capital letters, you are a mere salesperson, a broker. And that, except for great and reputable agents, is what makes this profession, more times than desirable, a "sea of blood." A place with lot of people that don't provide

13

the minimum added value. Everyone tries to do the same. Just mediate. They have become commodities. And therefore they are invisible people. White-label. They do the same as the rest. Do nothing special. They "kill" each other. **And a great players' agent has to add value, has to stand out for its professionalism, has to distance himself from the "sea of blood" to move to the "blue ocean".** He must be able to provide his client a great service from a multidisciplinary perspective. And for that **is mandatory continuous education.**

If you don't do that, if you don't get continuous education, you are doomed to constantly have to believe what other people tell you. Because you know absolutely nothing about what you are being told. And that's a bad thing.

If you pretend to be a good consultant you should always know what you are doing. Have such education that gives you sufficient criterion to determine whether what is happening or what you are being told is good, bad or susceptible of some modification. Otherwise, you are vulnerable to any issue you may be asked for. To anyone. And that may be the beginning of the end for your client and for you. There are countless cases of athletes absolutely ruined by issues that neither he nor his agent knew. Therefore, give good advice, learn continuously. You must know.

b. SELF-CONTROL

"The most powerful man is the one who is fully self-possessed". Aristoteles

Self-control is another key issue. It is impossible to advise your client well if you don't have this ability. You have to use up temperance and balance. You must know how to manage well the countless episodes of anxiety that you're bound to pass.

This job is characterized by the large number of waiting times. Of active standby. Don't forget that as an agent you're another link in this professional world. Very often, you may have to make many calls, write a huge number of emails and be forced to wait for replies and ratifications that never arrive. **This job is a job where you need to know how to wait**, you need to learn how to not despair, to know how to manage time to respect the thin line between being tenacious and being tiresome. And it's not an easy line to respect because often comes into play a huge enemy of this job called anxiety.

Sorry if in your case you suffer anxiety regularly, without going any further I had to learn to control it, but if you want to survive in this job you have to know how to handle it. You must know how to project a serene image, regardless that problems go inside. You have to keep your anxiety locked up. Don't let anxiety leave. If you do, anxiety will betray you and irremediably will affect your self-image and therefore your credibility. I insist, we must keep in mind this word: **credibility**. I'll repeat it more times in the future. It's a key issue.

c. <u>SELF-DISCIPLINE</u>

"The only discipline that lasts is self-discipline". Bum Phillips

As an autonomous agent nobody will tell you neither what to do, nor how you have to do it, nor if you're doing right or wrong, nor at what time you have to get up or go to bed, nor how many hours you have to spend, nor what games you have to watch, nor which players you have to see. Forget it. This doesn't work like that. It is you who has to organize and establish a roadmap. You and nobody else. And what's more difficult, you have to be committed to respect everything that you've considered, as well as trying to get the partial milestones that you have established along the way.

You won't have an "all-seeing eye" that will be marking guidelines and correcting you if understands that you are diverting. There is no such paternalistic figure that everyone hates when it exists and misses when it doesn't because you feel helpless. Don't look for approval because no one will give it to you. And if someone gives it to you, you should distrust, because he hasn't the slightest idea. Because if he would have it neither would have given you his approval, nor would have said it to you because that person, directly, would have done it already.

It is you, your confidence, your opinion, your goals and your roadmap. That's it. Did I mention that to do this job real passion is needed? I hope you're realizing about it as we go along. **Without passion the exercise of self-discipline is sterile**. However, if you overflow, passion, you'll banish forever excuses or justifications. Someone wisely said that **with excuses errors disappear**. If you want something go for it, don't just desire it. Set yourself a plan and go for it. Just that. But that plan must be set by you, in the time and the way you want, and with the changes you understand convenient. But all that under your responsibility. There is no oracle for it. Be mentally prepared.

d. <u>FRUSTRATION TOLERANCE</u>

Tom Watson, IBM founder said: *"If you want to succeed, double your failure rate"*. I would add: and don't succumb to them. In developing the commercial side of this job most times you fail. Deal with it. It is like that. But as I said earlier, Churchill said that success consists on going from failure to failure without loss of enthusiasm. I strongly agree.

The interesting thing of Churchill's claim is what you can read between lines. To go from failure to failure without loss of enthusiasm there is an inseparable and inherent thing to that assertion that Churchill didn't mention but leaves it sideways. And that is that to go from failure to failure its essential getting up each time you fail. Or, if you prefer, getting up after each frustration. It is true that frustration is expectation daughter. Expectations that, on the other hand, you contemplate for yourself. And that's the way it has to be. Because having expectations is an unequivocal sign that you have goals. And that's fine. But you have to know that the road is confusing.

The straight line rarely works. We must learn to overcome obstacles and to give curves. **The hard part is not doing. The hard part is being**. Being mentally prepared to know that frustrations are a very important variable, and that are very present, in this game. But that should not make us stop. You always achieve what you want if you have the willingness, determination and the courage not to falter until you succeed. But the road is hard and you have to be mentally prepared.

This could be summarized as follows, **"if it's not for you it won't be although you're in front, and if it's for you it will be although you get away"**. I hope you have it clear. Assume that there are variables you can't control. These variables generate anxiety and frustration. The best thing you can do is focus yourself on what depends solely on your performance. What has to be, will be.

e. PATIENCE PAYS..., AND SMART TENACITY AS WELL

One problem that exists when you have a series of objectives is that we tend to think that this objective is directly proportional to the work done by us. That is, I work that much, that much I get. And the truth is that this is a contradictory idea.

It is true that if you work hard your probability ratio tends to be higher, but this doesn't need to be so. Indeed I have never been absolutely in agreement with that established belief which says that everything is achieved through hard work. I really don't think so. **In what I believe is in working smart**, and that is not a direct result of working long hours. There we have the Pareto 80/20 law. **20% of the efforts generate 80% of results**.

Achieving goals is not only a matter of work (it is as well), it's rather a matter of psychology proper handling.

Businesses are not done by machines, businesses are done by people. Machines are mere instruments. So let's stop behaving as "instruments" and let's begin to use and work with what separates us from machines and which is our main distinguishing element: the brain. Think. Henry Ford said it clearly: ***"Thinking is the hardest work there is, that's why very few people do it"***.

This job has much to do with the ability to learn to wait. With the ability to realize that **sometimes the smartest thing is to do nothing**. Don't forget that you treat with people permanently. Thus, if you want to get a result that depends exclusively on people the main difference will be the kind of psychology you apply. Some people call it empathy.

You must be aware that once the "mechanical" work is done (calls, emails, meetings, visits, etc...), you have to know to wait, you have to be prepared to be willing to do anything except being patient. And for this anxiety management is essential.

Not being able to handle anxiety will lead you to hyperactivity. Hyperactivity only serves you to silence your inner critic and have the feeling that you are doing something. For some reason, people always have the feeling that everything has to rely on oneself. And it doesn't work like that.

The last thing you want to be for others is a bore. Be considered that has lot of adverse effects on self-image projection, and consequently on, guess what!, your **credibility**. This word again.

As you can see a great performance in this job has a lot to do with aptitude, but even more with attitude.

Maybe sometimes would be desirable to adopt a passive attitude but that doesn't mean that you should be idle. Nothing further from reality. It is about knowing how to manage time and respect the other. It is a matter of **"smart" tenacity, "thought" tenacity**. Let's say it is an "elaborate tenacity" rather than a "brute tenacity". If you manage to behave like this you'll have a lot done already.

Definitively, what is in your hand you have to do it perfectly. You have to know that not everything depends on you, that you deal with other people and that the best way to bear it is to be aware of it, to finish with anxiety and apply empathy. In the end this patience will pay you handsomely.

f.   <u>WHAT A SOCCER AGENT SHOULDN'T BE</u>

Let's play again the stock market game again. In the stock buying and selling market there is a figure you may know very well which is the broker. The broker is an intermediary who buys or sells on your behalf a series of stocks and charges a fee for it. It is an intermediary. That's it.

In my case, I don't like that definition of an agent as a simply intermediary. Some people do it, is respectable and there's nothing wrong with that. The only thing is that I don't understand this job that way. I don't want to simplify it this way.

I realize that with this topic I may enter into thorny terrain and possibly you don't share my opinion. I respect that. In my case, I understand this profession from a perspective that you may find overly romantic. But it's my vision. I understand a soccer agent as a companion, as a multidisciplinary counselor. Who knows a little of everything and possibly a lot about something in particular. With a great self-control.

But, why do we need to know a little of everything if we have the opportunity to ask for specialized counseling in a particular area (fiscal, labor, etc.)? Because you always have to have decisions under control. Choosing where to go also has to be a decision taken under control. And to make decisions like that you have to have a minimum knowledge of what you have up your sleeve. I'll insist on advising knowingly what for me it's crucial. There can be no gaps in the activity performance grounded in faith acts.

Whereupon, being properly prepared will help you, firstly, to define clearly what the subject is to, later, redirect it to those who may have a deeper knowledge of the subject. Secondly, and crucial in my opinion, to be able to evaluate the recommendations of these people from a critical perspective, and be able, if so, to do the right questions. So, you won't see yourself obliged to believe everything that someone can tell because you lack the basic knowledge that enables to be aware about what's going on.

I insist that **you have to avoid as far as possible faith acts in business**.

A good agent should be versatile, complete. A tennis player will never win if he doesn't know to backhand, no matter how good is your right. You must know how to manage yourself in all positions. If not, you will be a mere technical in a particular area, unable to cope in other areas.

With all this I'm referring to those who work as autonomous agents, not if you do it within a big agency. Big agencies work as a large corporate agent. The difference is that while in a one-person agent the multidisciplinary knowledge is included in himself, in company agents that multidisciplinary knowledge is divided in certain persons, such persons being, within their organization, more knowledgeable than others in certain aspects .

Agencies are another way to manage this activity. In fact there are some very important. Some will like them more, other less. The only issue that big agencies should pay attention to is the **ability to make their structures flexible** and therefore their activity. This element to be considered is enabled by a special cash flow, typical of this activity.

PART II – WHAT IS EXPECTED FROM A SOCCER AGENT

Everything and, at the same time, nothing. Everything depends on the area where you are moving and what kind of player you are working with. With the risk of generalizing too much I'll say that any player would tell you that it aims to play in the best team, be comfortable in the team and earn enough money in his sport career that allows him not having to work anymore and if possible, live at his best.

However, how do you do that? From there on it's your own task. What is important is having these principles clear, and from there apply all the ability and genius possible to generate sufficient tools to satisfy his desires.

At this point I can only remember Henry Ford's words when he said: *"If I had asked people what they wanted, they would have said faster horses"*. In similar terms Steve Jobs pronounced: *"People don't know what they want until you show it to them"*. Ultimately, your client will let you do whatever you think is ok, as long as you have the answers to their claims. He won't enter into whether or not it is orthodox. Any way of doing things will be welcome as long as it's respectful and meet your client objectives. Your client will not ask you for specific actions, he will ask you to solve his problems.

1. __PERSONAL BRANDING__

When we talk about personal branding we are talking about "personal get away". About the ability to be visible for the others, to get away from conventional. About highlighting oneself from the background. Definitively, about not being another one. About being different, in the best sense of the word.

This is a business concept transferred and applied to people. Why when you buy a product you choose one and not another? You do it because a certain brand transmits you higher reliability. And for that extra quality you don't mind paying an extra price. That particular brand transmits you a series of different values from the competition. Neither better nor worse. Just different. It is the final customer who will determine which elements of the different brands appreciate most.

The same could be applied to soccer agents. How can an individual become a personal brand?

Firstly, being a **great professional**. For that you must educate yourself. Permanently, constantly. Move away from our beliefs that ingrained idea that higher education is enough. Sorry, but not anymore. That paradigm has already passed away. If you don't try to improve every day and educate yourself you'll become someone absolutely outdated. Obsolete. **To improve your results it's imperative improving yourself**.

Secondly, you have to be **authentic**. Be yourself. Stay away from conventionalisms. Do not follow the guidelines of the "sheep". Follow yours. It is not desirable to be foreseeable. That only reflects being socially comfortable. Being different and attractive requires discomfort. Standing out from the well-known. It is mandatory to get out from labels from the preset vital attitudes. You are your own label. There is no one like you. **You have to put in value what you are**. That everyone can have clear who you are. What you offer. Authenticity.

Another very important element for a personal brand is **differentiation**. It is closely related to authenticity. When you are authentic, when you are you, and you have not been sucked into the "multitude" in the way of being and doing, you automatically differentiate yourself. Although it is a stagnant activity, with a determined "abc", a "how" can always exist that differentiates you. One way to do things. To relate yourself.

In this soccer agent activity there is a very particular and absolutely essential characteristic. A peculiarity that is absent in our day to day more times than desirable. And therefore, representing this characteristic is becoming a differential element. I'm talking about **honesty**. Be always honest. Don't ramble with that. Do not choose to be honest or not depending on the circumstances. Or depending on what you can lose. Be different. Be authentic. And most important: make the difference constant and enduring. If not you won't be reliable and you'll lose ... **credibility**. Again.

Third and finally you have to have **notoriety**. You need to be all the above and, also, you have to worry very much about making yourself visible, to make yourself relevant. It is useless to be different and authentic if nobody knows it. You must expose yourself, present yourself in society, your potential clients must know that you exist. For them, thus, to be aware of what you offer and if they like you, buy you.

Don't be afraid to fail. Don't be afraid to succeed! Trust yourself. Remove from your "mental software" the desire of others acceptance, approval. It is useless. In fact, it's the antithesis of what has been explained above.

2. <u>ONE-PERSON CONSULTANCY COMPANY VS AGENCY</u>

Generally, when you jump into this world you study, you pass an exam, you get the card and that's it. You start working. There are many books about it.

There are people who throw themselves directly and other who prefer starting their activity as an employee under the protection of an agency. Both methods are fine. Opting for one or the other is a matter of each personality. Of their propensity or aversion to risk. Obviously the maturation period of your activity as individual will be different depending on your election. It is also true that despite the fact that the sole agent requires a longer maturation period his learning process can be painfully greater. And I'm not referring to purely technical issues. I'm referring to **mental strength cultivation**, to **attention control and not drawing it away**.

Have your focus clear. Assume and deal with the swinging that will appear to keep yourself in the path. It is a superlative emotional learning. There is no protective umbrella. There is the trial and error.

Agencies are another thing. You can collaborate with them or directly be an employee. Thus learning is different. Can be less tiring from an emotional point of view. There is a protective shield to rely upon. There is always someone of your team that can help you. You directly learn the "know how". It's there. Within reach.

On the other hand, the skills you can learn may be predefined. That is, your level of learning is defined. The company policy can determine how far you can go. In which areas you are going to move on. Moreover, what things you can know and what things you can't.

That is why everyone must decide what their preferences are. They are different circumstances for different minds.

The foregoing regarding the beginning. However, there are others, of more entrepreneurial nature, that have to be taken into account when this activity is performed. I'll try not to exceed myself on purely technical issues and will try to make it understandable. It has to do with flexibility. But why do I talk about flexibility?

Sometimes flexibility is the key to success. It has to do with adaptability. It is closely linked to the structure, the structure of the activity costs.

In changing environments a fundamental element is the ability to make cost variable. There must be the possibility of making the structure more flexible. I'll try to explain it regarding soccer agents.

As we know, in general, the revenue stream in this activity is variable, undetermined. At least if it's compared to other sectors. For those players you have in the portfolio is more than possible that you have a recurring income from the contracts already signed. But in this world, what matters most is movement and the fact that it exists is not only up to your good work. There are issues that are beyond your control.

Therefore, that one-person agent will have greater flexibility to adapt himself to the sector situation. It will be more pliable, less rigid. He is less susceptible to market fluctuations, arriving at certain times to be more competitive. **The one-person agent sacrifices a larger volume for larger adaptability**.

Furthermore an agency will have an organization capable of developing such activity that is capable of carrying out a large business volume. However, they must be careful with fixing rigid structures which are little prone to flexibility. With a slow and costly adaptation process.

In good times, when a company consolidates fix costs its benefits are superior to those companies based on variable costs. However, they are more sensitive to activity changes. So that when the company wins, wins a lot but when the company loses, loses likewise.

Regarding the one-person agent when he wins he may not earn as much but when he loses his adaptation ability is bigger. Therefore, regardless the cost structure that is adopted for the activity development, a special emphasis on **adaptability** should be made. And for that reason, before that, I insist, before you do anything you have to know and consider very well the different scenarios that can occur, as well as the activity cash flows (revenues and expenses, and when they are produced).

3. <u>COMMERCIAL ISSUE</u>

"Customers are not tired of commercial arguments; they are tired of salespersons without arguments". Luis Folgado de Torres

Anytime you want to pick a player for your portfolio, pick that player with projection, interesting, at the time you approach and try to make him see that you are his best choice, always, I repeat, you will always have be prepared to answer a question. People will ask you that or not. But they will always be thinking about that, even in silence. The question is: Why you? I mean, what are you going to offer me that others won't.

One thing must be absolutely clear. What I call the **"social claim"**. Everyone is prone to want what others have wanted or have had before. Always. Nobody wants to make the first bet. Nobody wants to be the only one. And if he does, the added value that he has to perceive has to be far superior to those offered by others. Until the point to dispel his doubts. Therefore, in achieving customers, the degree of professionalism, creativity and differentiation must be important. Remember, why you?

Big agencies or big agents have an easy answer: because so and so-and-so is with me so I must be good. However, those starting should answer this question in the best way and as soon as possible. If you are not able to provide something different that is able to dispel the doubts of your clients, bad thing. We don't want to be in the "ocean of blood." Where everybody, because are equal, are skinned. We want to be in the "blue ocean". For that you have to define three clear advantages that you're going to provide your interlocutor. Neither two nor four. Three. Your interlocutor will not retain more. It's psychology.

Similarly, you should have prepared in advance a series of responses that can answer the following questions: **what, who, how, when, where and why**. Keep them ready. Do not improvise. If you improvise, you will doubt. And if you doubt you will generate distrust in your interlocutor. These doubts will be reflected in your personal projection. The distrust you generate affects your credibility. And without credibility you don't sell. **We must learn how to sell.**

I summarize what it is learned in a Master of Business Administration (MBA). **If you want to sell, or you do it better or you do it cheaper**. That's it. And whatever you choose, give it to understand to your interlocutor. Project it on each element of your behavior. I hope this is helpful for you.

4. <u>GOOD SOCCER PLAYERS SELL AND SELL THEMSELVES</u>

Despite what says in the title you have to know how to sell. Very important. **An agent has to be a strong seller**. And you won't sell well if you first don't know how to sell well. Everyone, absolutely everyone should learn how to sell. Dedicate a small portion of their time to learn the noble art of selling. No effort should be spared. Moreover, frequently your performance will be evaluated from a single viewpoint. My agent sells me well, or he doesn't? In a metaphorical sense, he talks well about the "horse"? Yes or no? Ultimately, gives results?

What is certain is that **advertising is the price you have to pay for not having a unique, remarkable product**. Just go out to the street to realize that the need for advertising and active selling is inversely proportional to the quality of your product. And the same happens in soccer. The sales effort that a "commodity" player requires is much higher than a, let's call it "crack", needs. Nothing surprising.

All this leads us to the next question. Saying all the above also leads to conclude that big players sell themselves alone. And they do it to the clubs themselves that would be, potentially, interested in having their services. But not only to those clubs. Also to the agents themselves! Agents fight over the player that stands out. If a player stands out immediately will have a crowd of people hanging around. All of them trying to sell their own benefits and talking about competition deficiencies. As I have said, an "ocean of blood". Everyone doing the same. Nothing different. Everyone offer themselves.

In this framework, if you're starting in this world you have two options: to offer something different or, if you don't have something different to offer or an innovative way to do it, desist. Directly. In which position can you be left by this? So that one who begins must differentiate the offer, ie differentiate himself, or just focus on what is less demanded (average soccer players). There is no other. It is the law of supply and demand. It is the only lasting law. It is the only natural law. Not written. Thus remains.

And guess what. If you are forced to keep what is less demanded you're obliged to increase your marketing skills. I insist you have to sell. Otherwise, redesign yourself and offer something or a way to do it that is different.

This business has a lot to do with a vicious circle. It is a kind of loop. If you are a well-known agent your reputation and your clients are your best marketing campaign. Your own clients speak highly of you. Inside the locker room itself. And there are many idle hours in hotels and concentrations. Therefore you won't seek clients. They will look for you. And that is the secret of success. Good players will come to require your services. You're doing well and your reputation is constantly feeding back and generating that triumphant flow.

On the contrary, if you're starting it will be very difficult for you to get the confidence of a player that is "tagged" so you won't have many opportunities to show your talent, which will cause you a lack of reputation. And with no reputation you won't generate enough confidence to the players you are interested in. This is the loop that's not interesting. At some point you have to break that recurrent circle. And that circle is broken by specific matters: a player who stands out at a certain time without anybody expecting it, a player that for any reason trusts you more than another and that afterwards stands out, etc.

What must be kept in mind is that luck has to be sought. With learning, work and "smart" tenacity. **Luck is the point where preparation and opportunity converge**. What can't be is not having preparation when opportunity arrives. That is within our control. Let's use the opportunity to constantly improve. The opposite would be a terrible and expensive mistake in the long run.

5. NOTORIETY AND VISIBILITY

This topic is a subject that is becoming recurrent, but is very important. **A player wants you to make him feel special and wants you to project that specialty to others**. You won't do well unless you don't apply these principles to your own person. To sell something to your prospect don't tell him, show it to him. And show it to him by yourself. Give notoriety and visibility to yourself. Be your own advertising campaign. **Become a personal brand**. Contrast yourself. Separate yourself from the background. Outline yourself. Be yourself what you shout about. As Woody Allen said: *"Things have to be done, not to be said, because when you do them they are said by themselves"*.

6. CONTACTS: A TIME AND DEDICATION ISSUE

It is very common to hear that an agent is very good because he has many contacts. Let's not fool ourselves. Having contacts as such is a matter of time and dedication.

Do not confuse the terms. When we say that an agent has contacts is true that he has them, but what he really has is credibility.

Having contacts is a summation of names and phone numbers. It's not about the contacts, but what you do with the contacts and how you present yourself to them. There is no point in having a Ferrari if you can't drive it.

Contacts are people you should work with. Things are there to be used, but to use them well. There are many people who boast because of their contacts. As if that did any good. That's the beginning of the road, but there is a lot more. What matters is what you do with that data. And even more, what is really interesting is what type of relationship you are going to establish with them and what you are going to do to make that happen. **The ultimate goal is to establish trusty relationships**.

It is preferable to have a modest network of contacts but perfectly worked where you are recognized as someone reliable and respectable, to collect numbers for the simple fact of having them. As if they were trading cards. That doesn't lead to anything.

Instead of compile data systematically is more interesting, regarding this, to establish trusting relationships with your peers, ie other agents to, by networking, do business from trust, from credibility. Although they are not done directly by you, yes through another agent that can have that relationship of trust with the end client. Formulas to regulate that exist. And many.

7. <u>RELATIONSHIPS AND SELLING TECHNIQUES</u>

The great big question you may be asking yourself is: "OK, selling is crucial but, **how do you sell well**? What do I have to pay special attention to? Well, the answer is simple. **We must begin closing the mouth and opening the ears**.

The main element of selling is knowing what the other wants. To practice an "active listening". What you want doesn't matter. No one is here to listen to us. Absolutely no one. Everyone cares only and exclusively about theirs. The rest goes into one ear and gets out the other. Therefore we must focus on our interlocutor needs. The more attention we pay to what someone else tells us the better effect we will cause in the other. He will know that we care about him, and that will improve his attitude towards us and, also, his willingness to do business. He won't have the feeling that we are there to sell him something.

First listen and then offer. It is useless to offer a person a four-wheel drive, for example, when he is crazy about buying a sports car. Therefore, first listen.

As I said, it is strictly necessary to open up your ears and let the other person talk. If we let him he will end up giving us clues about their interests and what he wants. **I encourage paying special attention to the "last drop" of what our interlocutor says. It is often the most revealing**.

Once you have heard his point of view, and after having drawn conclusions on what may be his interests and motivations, we must meet the following three steps:

We must first **catch his eye**. The client needs to understand that you are a person able to deal with his problems and concerns.

Let him talk and listen. It is after hearing what he has to say when we have to throw the message to get his attention. Our partner has to look at us. And for that it has to be a relationship between what the other person transmits us and what we are going to suggest. **Usually, while the other person speaks, we are more aware of what we are going to say next than what the other person is telling us. As a result, there is usually no connection between what we say and what has been transmitted to us. Dissociation occurs**.

Second, once our interlocutor attention is captured we have to **raise his interest**. This requires that the interlocutor has paid attention to us previously. **There is no possibility**

to raise interest without previously having captured attention.

We must have clear that people, all of them, will just show interest in us if we are going to report them a profit or if we are going to solve them a problem. Don't fool ourselves. They are the only two ways by which a person will see his interest stimulated. Thus, when selling we need to have perfectly clear what we are going to say our interlocutor and, more important, how are we going to say it.

The interlocutor has to have clear, in a transparent way, that the message you're sending him will benefit him in some way or will solve him a problem. That is, it must be clear that he is going to get any benefit over a real issue that concerns today.

Third and last, it's not enough to say things to our interlocutor. We must show that we don't lie and that what we are saying is true. The **demonstration** must be done once the interlocutor has shown interest. It makes no sense to do that before. It will fall on deaf ears. It's useless.

On the other hand, we have to be especially aware of the sale scenario. We have to worry for the scenario in which communication is going to be developed. Has to be a scenario of collaboration and a peaceful atmosphere. The opposite would be counterproductive.

We have to look after, not only the message content, but also the form of the message. Let's focus on being simple. Let's simplify. We have to make sure that the other part has understood the message that is intended to be communicated.

Repeating in other way the message is another consideration to keep in mind. That helps to position it in the mind of our interlocutor.

It would be great as well to have convincing examples of what you're communicating. Any help will be welcome. All these issues make persuasive communication easier.

And, more important, under any concept despise, be intolerant or waste your interlocutor's time. It will only lead to the opposite effect. It is not interesting to fall out with anyone because you never know if in the future, and because of other issues, we will meet with the same person. Let's be cautious in this regard.

8. CREDIBILITY

Albert Einstein said: ***"Whoever is careless with the truth in small things, is not trustworthy on important issues".***

Credibility is the business fundamental element. The most important thing we've talk about so far. Without credibility you're nobody. Neither as agent nor as nothing.

The search for credibility affects everything else. The ultimate goal of each of the things you need to take care of and pay attention to is the pursuit of credibility. And that, for your audience, entails becoming a brand. **We could say that credibility is equal to brand generation**.

In addition, this credibility builds your reputation. Oprah Winfrey said: "In the end, what you have is your reputation". The trust that the market deposits in you has to do directly with your brand or your reputation. Take care of it as if it was your greatest treasure. Don't trivialize on this topic. I won't stop repeating it. Your reputation is like the bread crumbs that you're leaving behind. People hate uncertainty. People look for foreseeable and predictable things. Therefore, **first produce and then manage a career of positive predictability**. It takes years to get it but it's mandatory to get it. When you say you'll do something, do it. When you say you're going to call, call. Fulfill your commitments. Always. Although it may seem that you won't get a direct benefit in the short term, it doesn't matter, do it. Commit yourself with your commitments. It's worthy in the long run. It is a distance race. Your credibility and reputation are your best business cards. They will talk for you even without you. They will generate a flow of word of mouth.

Apply the "ten year rule". This rule says that in circumstances where you do not know what to do, where to go, think about the following: "In ten years, what would make me happy to have done? The decision you make will always be correct.

Be coherent. There has to be no discrepancy between what you say and what you do. And what you say always do it. There can't be differences between your intentions and your behavior. Warren Buffet used to say, *"I look for three things when hiring someone. The first is personal integrity. Second is intelligence and the third, a high level of energy. But if you don't have the first one the other two end up killing you"*. That's it. You need to have a basis of principles and values. Live under them. And transmit them.

What you do is more important than what you say, but even more important than what you do are those facts interpretations. **The most crucial are not the facts but the interpretations of those facts**.

Everyone synthesizes everything they see and hear based on their "mental map". Their paradigms. Therefore, credibility is closely linked to what each person thinks are the priorities of the opposite. **It's not what you do, it's what the other person thinks you do**. Are the intentions our counterpart thinks we have that will determine his behavior. It is not about the real intentions. It is about the imagined intentions. **And the person (or your potential client) will believe you have some intentions and not others depending on what he thinks your motivations are**.

Therefore, take care of this aspect. Worry about the interests that move the other part. As a soccer agent, is not the same that your potential client thinks your motivation is to make money, rather than help. Remember that no one cares about you. Only cares about his own. Focus on helping and they will help you. But do it for real. People always detect impostors. And help with proper behavior. **Behavior continues to be the manifestation of intentions and priorities**.

More issues. Capable people inspire, so cultivate yourself permanently. There is no expiration date for learning. Recycling must be constant. As David Maister said: *"Knowledge and skills, as all assets, are devalued with surprising speed"*. And you are your greatest asset. Take advantage of your strengths. Strengthen them even more, and set a goal for yourself. Set with determination where to go. Where are you going. And commit yourself to your goal!

In the event that meeting your commitments costs you very much, focus on increasing your integrity, on paying special attention to mutual benefit. When you adopt this way of learning, do it repeatedly. Thus, it will end up becoming a habit.

9. __NEGOTIATION__

"The most important thing in a negotiation is to hear what is not said". Peter Drucker

Negotiation in soccer has very showy and typical issues. Generally in negotiation scenarios there is a person who wants something in certain conditions and another willing to give it in exchange of other conditions, which generally don't agree with those of the potential buyer. Therefore, the negotiation is about reaching an agreement point. Nothing new.

Well, in soccer very often, indeed I would say almost always, this is not usually the case. **In soccer there is a club that wants to buy, but there is a club, that doesn't want to sell!** Have you ever stopped to think about the degree of difficulty that this involve? How can you negotiate with someone when he does not want to get rid of an asset? Therein lies the difficulty.

Let's also add that the transaction object is not an inert being, is a human being, a thinking person, who has his own view of everything around and someone who is not moving alone. He has family, wife and children, with everything all that entails: change the residence country, habits, friends, school, etc. It is not an easy thing. The player will simply want his conditions to be improved in such way that deserves all disadvantages. For normal people is an additional stress to consider the possibility of a180 degree turn in your life. With a player happens the same.

So let's recap. We have a scenario where there are the buyer club, the seller club (which doesn't want to sell), the player with his whole family (who just wants to improve and don't be messed around) and the agent.

And what is your role as agent in all this issue? **Your role as an agent is being the lubricant, the greaser, the emotions moderator**. In these situations you have to not only look after the interests of your client, that you have to, but to make those clients desires come true you need to perform a hard work of engagement between the different parties. Wax on, wax off, that would say Mr. Miyagi on Karate Kid.

Don't forget that the buyer wants to sign a player paying as little as possible and the seller, not only doesn't want to sell high, very often directly he doesn't want to sell! And the player interested in improving and in not being disturbed.

Usually it is thought that in a negotiation you must join requests, positions, if preferred, when in fact it is not. **What you really have to reconcile are interests**. Requests and positions are the result of interests.

In a lot of cases negotiations break off because people persist in requests rather than deal with interests. Actually, what you need to ask yourself is: Why is this person asking me that? Why that person doesn't want to give me this?

Negotiation is a trading game. When a person accepts, directly, a request, it is not a negotiation, that's another thing. Call it acceptance, surrender, whatever you want. Negotiating is trading. **And in this trading game asking is crucial.**

First, you have to ask to go beyond the requests. So you can know what interests motivate those requests. Perhaps those interests can be satisfied with other issues that you can offer. You have to ask. **The one who asks, leads**.

In many occasions by simply asking the other party releases information, that otherwise he would never have told you, and that is essential for knowing the underlying interests. Let them talk, talk until the end.

Neither has to be only a matter of price. When you face a negotiation **you must be as flexible as possible**. If you sit at a negotiating table with a single negotiable variable, price, the negotiation rigidity will be absolute and quite possibly will stagnate. Or even worse, you'll enter into what is commonly known as haggling. That's not interesting. That's not negotiate. That's succumbing to the interest of the other without paying attention to your own interests. You will leave the negotiation table and the other will have won. And, therefore, you will be dissatisfied because you will realize that you have lost.

It is not about winning or losing, it's about both parties having the feeling of having won. And that is achieved by the exchange of negotiable variables. Price is one, but there are plenty of them. You just have to be creative to prepare a list with several negotiable variables in a priority order, from most to least important. And having perfectly clear in which range you can move with each of the variables. So that when negotiating you can use that variables successively as you go through the negotiation.

There may be variables that you are not interested in exchanging. If so, skip to the next variable in the list. In many times you will be in situations where you have real interest in an issue that is very important for you and you find out that the other party is giving it to you in exchange for something that is not important for you at all. This happens a lot.

Negotiations are won before sitting down, not on the negotiation table. Prepare the strategy before, filling as much as possible your list of negotiable variables, so that nothing can catch you by surprise and that the creativity fostered in the preparation let you get out of specific situations that may be enclosed.

There are three vital concepts: preparation, preparation and preparation. If you act on the way you won't ever know what you want, or how to get it, so you'll humble yourself to other party without realizing you're losing with the operation.

So, as an agent you have to have very clear what are the interests of each party in the negotiation. The buyer wants to buy a player. The request is the player but the interest may be reinforcing a position. The seller club doesn't want to sell. It is possible it may request the other club stop trying to buy the player. However, its interest may be that it is no able to have in the short term, and at an affordable price, a player for replacement. After that you might find the player who may be reluctant to change club for "only" a great wage raise. It is possible that his concern is not only the money. He may be concerned about his family and where he might live at his new club, which school his child will attend to and what kind of life his wife may have. That is, in the case of the player if it's only about the salary he may not be interested. However, for a lower wage increase but an improvement in other conditions; school, house, residential area, etc., the player might change. But in order to know this we must ask. I insist.

If the seller doesn't want to get rid of his player because of its inability to find someone else, you as agent can find solutions to respond to that interest, which is not a request, to create a situation where the club might be more open to sell the player.

Similarly, if the buying club is interested in knowing which is the underlying interest of the selling club which has motivated it's not selling decision, the club may adopt more or less creative solutions, including a number of players in the transfer, for example, that can give solutions to those interests that support the requests.

If we talk about money and, for example, a club asks for 20 and the other offers 15, it is possible that the reason for disagreement is not purely a matter of numbers. You should ask and get the interest. It is good to know why a club doesn't want to give more than 15 and the other won't accept less than 20. We can have the situation where a club can't offer more than 15 now because it is involved in other transfer operations, although the club could offer it later. We would then be talking about a problem of terms, not numbers. Therefore, once the underlying interest it's known, the selling club could accommodate itself to this new reality and include additional clauses that would allow to combine interests, as varying amounts depending on goals, gains rate of future transfers, etc.

On the opposite side, it is possible that behind a request of 20 there is an interest that goes beyond the player itself who is the transfer object. It may be the case that with that amount the club is considering the possibility of dealing with the purchase of a player who plays on a third team, and that this third team is asking for that amount. And here is where you could get in as an agent. How? Searching a player for that third team, according to its aspiration, that can allow a more flexible position of the club on its demand. Which, in turn, will cause a decrease in the request of the second club, making viable to approximate its initial request from 20 to the offered price of 15. Do you think that's a good solution? Got that?

I reiterate that to know reality you must deepen. And that is done through questions.

As seen, is a matter of preparation. It is a key thing. A creativity issue. That is, look for negotiable and interchangeable units.

At this point you should be calm. That is, do not mix the professional with the personal. Do not be influenced by other party positions. One thing are the positions that are taken and another the person. Do not mix that and everything will be ok.

And it is also true that it is also a matter of time. Time can be your greatest ally and your greatest enemy. Indistinctly. It will be your enemy when you negotiate with haste. The one who has no need to hurry has a point in his favor. Never negotiate with urgency. Never accept other party's positions that force you or invite you to make quick decisions.

It is not about developing here all negotiation techniques either. There are many books about it. My goal is simply to provide a series of touches that can be helpful for you and that will serve you to clarify a little more the specifics of this subject in the agent profession.

10. <u>CONTRACTS</u>

A contract can be verbal or written. Samuel Goldwyn said: *"A verbal contract is not worth the paper where it is written"*. Therefore, I will listen and I will refer to written contracts. About what? Soccer player contracts. About which variables? About whatever you want. There are type issues that are in every soccer contract. However, for everything else, as you want. Creativity power. We would enter into what is purely contract negotiation.

A contract between a club and a player is a contingency contract. Absolutely. A contingency contract would be, in a colloquial sense, a contract as **"if this, then that"**. I'll explain why this is like that.

Except for type issues, ie names, wage, cancellation clause (in Spain), courts, etc.., practically all clauses that are introduced are contingency clauses.

It is true that players and coaches want to ensure a minimum for themselves. However, the position of the club must also pay attention to other issues. A club can have an idea of the performance that the player will have. But no one knows it for sure. Therefore, a number of variable clauses, that can suppose a great increase for the player but which are well suited to contingencies, are included. So many goals, so much more. If you get the Ballon D'Or, so much more. And so on and so forth.

The player salary increase is closely related to how his performance affects the club's treasury. In relation to sports results, advertising, and increases associated with the player professional notoriety growth.

Beyond these issues, the variables that can be negotiated, which will have as result the respective clauses, tend to infinity. Absolutely everything can be negotiated. Flexibility in these variables is crucial.

In this regard, I make special emphasis on the cancellation clauses. A variable that is highly susceptible to flexibility, although this way of understanding it is not very common. A flexibility conditioned to performance, to which, moreover, also depend directly other variables. Why the cancellation clause must be a fixed amount? The clauses are closely related to the contract and the player value. Therefore, on a contingency contract, it is presumably that the lower performance, the lower wage, and, consequently, with a lower wage the value of the amount of the cancellation clause would also have to be reduced.

If such cancellation clause is closely linked to a contract of variables that fluctuates with the performance of the player, the clause should also fluctuate accordingly. It would have to be associated with the achievements and performance of the player, as do the contract clauses. If the player does well, the clause goes up, if he does bad, goes down.

It is similar in case of injury. A player value can't be the same if he plays and stands out that if he passes all the season injured.

The rigidity of cancellation clauses is, for me, out of season. Its inclusion would also have to include a unilateral break up clause for the club. And not always happens.

In conclusion, regarding contracts it's all about how creative each of the parties are, as I mentioned in the previous chapter.

However, I want to talk to you about one thing that I find interesting. It is only a suggestion. **It is about that, as far as possible, you should try to minimize the negotiable units**. Negotiate according to minutes, rather than games. Negotiate according to games, rather than five block games. And so for all those questions that you consider appropriate. As in the "normal" world where is better to negotiate according to days rather than months, as well as hours rather than days. Usually when you tend to minimize the negotiable units the resulting final figure is usually higher. There are cases of all kinds, but this is normally the case. Hairdressers know that very well when they add to the final price small issues that raise the price of the product: shampoo, vitamins, conditioner, etc.

11. <u>SIDE ACTIVITIES</u>

With side activities I refer to issues such as advertising and image rights. Usually image rights contracts that a club makes with a player have a dual purpose. On one hand pretend to reach a certain net salary for the player with the lowest possible tax cost. Remember that regarding this the player would be taxed on the corporate income tax rather than the personal income tax. These contracts are usually performed with commercial companies owned by the player himself. In recent years, special attention is being paid to this maneuver by authorities, and modifications have been made establishing the limits allowed to be paid for this concept (Spain). But I will not bore you with all these things. It would be better to leave it for another time.

On the other hand, the reason why the image rights between the club and the player are negotiated responds to a simple reason. The club believes that the player will benefit from the advertising point of view for the simple reason of being the player part of the club. Therefore, the club understands that the fairest thing is to receive as well a portion of that pie as compensation. The club sees that as one more element that facilitates their ROI (Return on Investment). The club recovers part of the investment through the revenue associated with the player's image through advertising and image contracts.

I advise you to pay special attention to the fiscal connotations derived from image rights. It is well known that these days these issues are followed with particular diligence by the authorities in order to prevent fraud.

As an agent who advises people that have some popularity, you should notice that **the degree of visibility of your client is directly proportional to the degree of social and fiscal responsibility your client must have**. As a result, we must increase the level of alert with such matters. Do not forget that the soccer stars you advise are located in the apex of the pyramid. They are the tip of the iceberg. Very often they act as a decoy for authorities that see these people's profile inspections as the perfect target to be exemplary. You have to be especially aware of this. The opposite would be very unprofessional.

Take care of the details and the overall image that you project, both you and your client.

12. <u>WEALTH MANAGEMENT</u>

When I read things like the ones I'm going to say I reach the inevitable conclusion that something is being done in the wrong way. That there is something we have to change.

But not only that. In fact I am among those who think that, usually, people who are part of this world haven't got the slightest idea of what is happening actually.

Ignorance, selfishness and shortsightedness are soccer players' intimate enemies. Individualism and the short-term are temptations that circle them. **According to a Schips Finanz study 30% of active players are ruined and 50% are ruined when his career ends**. It may seem surprising to some but it is not.

When we talk about soccer players we talk generally about people that a very early age, many of them, all of a sudden make lots of money. And having the pockets full very often clouds the vision and makes many players get blinded and lose perspective. Short-termism and hedonism seize them. As bad as having anything is having a lot and not having the slightest capacity to manage it. Usually when one is not aware of the effort involved in earning money tends to squander it away equally.

The poor financial education that usually soccer players have does not help either, and that ignorance acts as a lure for some bad companies, which present themselves as experienced advisers or investors and dupe players with the intention of doing business ... for them.

I'll insist whatever is necessary on defending my personal point of view that, despite not having to be nor law specialist, nor labor specialist, nor financial specialists, is crucial that players have a general "bath" in all these issues in order to avoid bad passages that occur more times than desirable.

So in these lines I'll try to give you an overview of what should be an appropriate and profitable wealth management considering the long-term. I'll try not to be too technical even though sometimes it may seem so. I apologize for this in advance. However, I feel it is vital to expose certain considerations here that, I'm sure, will be very profitable for your clients' asset management and for your personal finances as well.

Everyone is aware that the duration of an athlete's career is very short compared to other conventional careers. You know it and everyone knows it. This being so, this idea should be in the subconscious of any good consultant. And I go further. It should also be installed on your client's subconscious. Choose the right way to do it: through the "light rain" (reduced doses given in a recurrent way), being annoying, well, the way you understand its better. But don't forget that the ultimate goal should be positioning this idea in everyone's mind. It is important to do so because this idea affects everything else.

According to this, it can't be thought that if a player, for example, earns two million dollars a year this figure corresponds to their annual income. Well. It is true that it is, but not entirely. I'll try to explain this below.

The annual income of a soccer player, because of his short career, in order to record them in the right way from the practical point of view should be deferred in time. Life expectancy in men is around 80 years old. However, it is yet to see the player who reaches that age still playing. Therefore, attributing the income to the fiscal year in which it is obtained could enter into what might be called fiction. Yes, you heard right. Fiction. The reality is that it shouldn't be like that.

I don't pretend to change with this all your paradigms. Nothing could be further from the truth. I just want to explain you what I think. As a Schips study points out about 30% of active players is ruined. You may still wonder, but how can be that if many of them earn millions and the others don't earn a bad salary? Saying that means that ordinary mortals are also ruined? Well I'll tell you something. No. It has nothing to do with it. But absolutely nothing. **A great income doesn't mean you are rich!** Far from that.

Wealth has more to do with the amount you spend (and you keep), rather than with the amount you earn. Wealth has to do mainly with financial freedom. It's all about time. I'll explain you.

A wealth definition could be the time you can live with your regular monthly expenses if you stopped working today. That's why wealth is measured in days, months or years.

A person that earns millions can be poor. If you earn two million annually but you spend 2.2 million we can say that your wealth is negative. Moreover, if your spending level is 1.8 you'll enter into the "middle" class. Why? Because your wealth would be almost of a month. That is, if you stop working today you would only have money for a month according to your monthly expenses. Surprised? Well, there's more.

The normal employee usually behaves similarly with the revenue obtained. He can earn 1000 and spend 1200, or spend 800. But the level of wealth compared to the soccer player remains similar, regardless the great income disparity between them. There is also another issue. It could be said that with the same income/expenditure ratio the wealth degree tends to be higher in a normal person than in a soccer player because of a simple question. While a normal person works permanently until the age of retirement, the sporting life of a soccer player finishes just a little over 30 years old. So his annual income, unlike ordinary people income, should be deferred in time. It is an income in a relatively short period of time that should be enough for the rest of his days.

Many soccer players either don't understand this, or don't want to understand. And what's even worse, many of his advisers ignore this issue because they think that while his client gives him profit, there is no reason to be concerned about the future. That is a matter of the player, they think. In their opinion, as an agent, you can work in the future with new young players. That's the way many of them think. I ask you please not to be one of those.

Ok but, all this about making incomes and money last, how do you do it? I'll try to give you a clue.

This is where you, as a responsible agent, must play a major role. To explain it, first I would like to describe you what does a common employee with his income.

As an employee example I'll take those who tend to poverty and those who might belong to the middle class.

Let's say that when a poor employee gets his payroll (income) he spend it practically all on living expenses like water, electricity, food, clothes, etc. I hope everything is perfectly clear until now.

Employed people who belong to the middle class have a slightly different behavior. A middle class employee when gets the income does two things primarily. First, like poor people, puts money aside for expenses. Secondly, puts money aside for liabilities: car, house, credit card, etc.

No. I'm not wrong. The house and the car are not assets, as everyone thinks. In fact, they are generally liabilities. Therein lies the importance of financial education. And you, as a good agent, and in order to advise properly your clients, should have a minimum of this education.

To let things more or less clear I'll tell you that for practical purposes, not accounting purposes, **an asset is anything that puts money in your pocket and a liability is anything that takes money out of your pocket.**

Thereby, when you purchase a house, what you're really doing is purchasing a liability because that house is taking money out of your pocket every month. The same thing happens with the car. When you buy a car what you're doing is purchasing a liability because the car credit will remove money from your pocket every month.

A house will only be an asset when the cash-flow that supplies is higher than the expenses. That is, when you buy a house and you put it for rent, your house will be an asset because it puts money every month in your pocket, as long as there is a positive difference between what you earn from the rental and the expenses that such property will suppose. Similarly, a car will be an asset if you rent it and get a regular income, higher than the expenses involved.

A house with mortgage that is not rented will always be a liability. People can say it's an asset because you can sell it. But what is certain is that while the requested mortgage is blocked and it's unchangeable, the price of the property may fluctuate. So, you can run the risk of being in a downward economic situation and be forced to sell the house. In this case there is a risk of getting for the house a lower amount than the obligation acquired. With the additional point that when you hire a mortgage you can pay even double the price of the house depending on the payable interests. You have to be careful with that.

When a middle class person buys a house usually does so through a mortgage, and acquires it to live in it. Therefore it is a liability because it does not generate any positive cash-flow for your pocket. The same thing happens with the car and other luxury items that soccer players usually acquire as big brand clothes, watches etc.

Therefore, as I have said, a middle class person puts aside his monthly payroll for habitual maintenance costs and for the acquisition of liabilities, as the things he acquired do not put money in his pockets but they remove it.

What conclusion can be drawn from this? What we could get clear is that these people will never be rich. Not because of their income level, which can be very important, but because of their financial paradigm and its spending pattern. Whatever their incomes are they are a few months away from bankruptcy, because the higher the income level is the higher the expenses are. So we are always at the same point. It is a fallacy to think that financial problems are fixed with more revenues. In fact is often the opposite, they get worse.

The mere possibility that almost everyone is a few months far from financial collapse means that virtually anybody has financial freedom. What I mean is, hardly anyone is in the position of not having to worry about where the next dollar is going to come from. Many are bound to work for money, at least until retirement (if they can retire). I say at least because one thing is the legal retirement age and another is the retirement real age. It is pointless that the state tells me that I can retire at the age of 67 if I can hardly live with the pension. That is, I will need to find another job, even if it is part time to supplement my pension. If not, it will be tough.

So we have, firstly, the regular employees who spend more than what they earn, or virtually everything that they earn, and, what is more, they also spend it on liabilities. And secondly, the players that earning even infinitely more than a normal employee spend as well the money in acquiring liabilities. With a few months wealth as well and with an important aggravating factor: that from a certain age will no longer earn these amounts and that they still have a lifetime ahead and with an uncontrolled spending habit that will lead them to bankruptcy. We could conclude that they are even worse.

I hope that so far everything is clear. In the following lines I'll explain what you should do, in general, and in soccer counseling, in particular.

To make possible that players can live the rest of their lives with what they have won during their sport career the following has to be done.

On one hand, and the easiest thing, is to convince the player to be professional in his **personal care**, relating food and rest, with the goal of extending as much as possible the flow of extra revenue. It is not the same that your client retires at 28 that at 40. You can ask Paolo Maldini. That's a good issue but it is not the only one.

On the other hand you have to work with the players in a **good financial plan**. The objective is no other than to obtain the player financial freedom once it is retired and no longer active in soccer.

For that it is crucial to know where the revenues that we are going to spend or invest come from. Most often, the money we spend or invest comes from our usual source of incomes, the payroll. In the case of soccer players is not different. The quantities change but not the pattern. We can say that both employees and players spend or invest the money that comes from their "active" work.

What I mean by active work? I refer to those revenues in which it's compulsory that you are there for

them to be generated. An employee has to go to his work place to work. A player has to train and play matches. Similarly, in advertising terms, a player, generally, must attend and record the corresponding spot to collect the money of a campaign. That's what I mean by active income. You have to be there to collect it.

These revenues will never give you the financial freedom we pursue as good agents we are. Neither to the traditional employee nor the soccer player. One day the player will stop playing and then what. Where are the revenues going to come from?

It is very possible that you may be thinking right now that the player has possibly invested or could in the future sell some properties of what he thinks are assets, but as I said before they can be so or not.

If you buy a house and you expect the price to rise in order to sell it and get a gain. That's all right. Everyone does that. We call this capital gain. It's an extraordinary profit of a given amount. But that is not what I'll seek.

I prefer, and hopefully I'll convince you, what is commonly understood as capital flow. What is the difference between capital gain and capital flow? As I explained you on a property sale profit could be a capital gain. Buy cheap. Sell expensive. I get a profit.

However, if instead of selling the house with the intention of obtaining a gain you rent it to get an income, that income would be what we call cash-flow. And that flow will be positive if the rental income exceeds all the costs of the property (mortgage, insurance, repairs, unpaid wages, etc.).

For me it's much more interesting this second option. Don't you think the same? Why? Because, firstly, if you rent a house the possibility of a future capital gain remains. This option does not extinguish the other. Secondly, and this is what I find most interesting, the rental income is a "passive" income.

What is passive income? Well unlike active income, **a passive income is the one you get in a recurrent way and indefinitely with no need to go to work.** When you rent a house you get an income every month without having to be working. At first you'll need to do some work to rent the apartment, but once rented income comes alone in a recurrent way. The royalty rights, like in books, songs, etc. behave similar. A more or less important initial work is required but then, once done, the income is obtained whether you work or not, whether you are there or not, whether you are in a country or in another, or even being at the beach. A passive income can be obtained 24 hours a day, 365 days a year.

In fact they are the only way to get financial freedom. Throughout passive incomes. Not through active incomes. You might like your job and you might like as well get active incomes. That's fine. But this way you'll never get financial freedom because revenues depend on your performance, and the effort is limited and so do the days. It is to be seen the day with more than 24 hours. Therefore, **you will have financial freedom when your passive incomes exceed your expenses.**

Is getting clearer what is the secret? It is not about earning a lot. It is more about being conscious of your expenses and how revenues are generated. The way you decide to get them. Through your own activity: active income, or through your assets: passive income.

This passive income generates a recurring and potentially infinite cash-flow. Passive income is earned through assets. An asset is your own business, a book, a song, shares, etc. On balance, anything that puts money in your pocket. It is not the amount that goes into your pocket, but what causes the money to go there.

Your client in order to get financial freedom has to be able to earn passive income that generates permanent and recurring cash-flow. This is not possible if there are no assets. Therefore, **you have to collect well understood assets. That generate rent, cash-flow**.

But what usually happens is that people don´t focus on assets creation or acquisition. They put aside their work income for expenses or acquisition of liabilities which turn in more expense. Lot of people seems to have money but they are actually poorer than the poor themselves. Many people buy luxury liabilities such as yachts and cars, through credit, which in the end will increase debt and their income will go permanently to pay off debt.

What I recommend, both you and your clients, is that instead of buying things, which are mere expense, acquire assets with the revenues made. Assets that generate cash-flow. Rent. That generate passive income. With the passive income that you'll be obtaining put aside money for regular expenses and save the rest to investment in new assets that will generate more flow and more passive income. And so on and so forth. Luxuries will come later. **What is convenient is first generate the passive income stream that enables treating yourself. And not before.**

If your client, as is entering money for his sport activity, puts aside money for collecting assets that generate a passive cash-flow where part of it can be reinvested in more assets, rather than spending money purchasing liabilities (such as cars and unnecessary luxuries), you'll get your client the possibility to acquire luxuries with the income generated by their assets through cash flow, not through his sport activity. Then, only then he will be able to buy luxuries without compromising his financial freedom. Everyone should have this issue into account.

No one can be rich, no matter the money he may earn, if his income depends only on his active work because that income is delimited and has an expiration date. This is what many players do not know or don't want to know. And what many advisers moving around don't know or interestedly don't tell his clients. In order that our client acquires financial freedom once his career is finished the only existing road is the one I've just discussed. There is no other. Now you know it.

You have also to pay special attention to the assets in which your client invests. We should not invest in issues that we don't know about. Many players lose huge amounts of money because they put their money in risky and unknown investments. Because of things they've heard. They just trust what they are told. As they don't know, they are forced to believe everything that those in whom they have placed their trust tell them. That's why getting the player's confidence, no matter how, is the key for everything else. Unfortunately, ignorance always has a negative impact on those people who are naive. And where it hurts most: in the wallet.

13. <u>SOCCER RETIREMENT</u>

For a soccer player the retirement concept is something that causes true vertigo. Few players are comfortable as the "edge of the precipice" approaches. Retirement is something every player prefers to ignore, as if it wouldn't exist. It is one of the main reasons of self-deception. But denying it doesn't mean that it is not. And that fear shouldn't exist. I can only think that it exists because they haven't done things well in advance.

It is true that what is unknown causes some anxiety. True. However, I think that the fear that retirement causes in any soccer player implies some apprehension to leave behind all that good stuff of the profession, which the soccer player believes is going to lose. I can come to understand it. But there is no reason why these things have to disappear.

Retire from soccer should only mean stop kicking a ball, but the economic benefits should continue. It should not be otherwise. If things, financially speaking, have been done well over the player's sports career, his financial freedom should be absolutely guaranteed. As well as whims, why not say it.

To banish the retirement fear in any player, firstly, review the immediately preceding paragraphs that talk about financial planning. And secondly, stop thinking that our retirement well-being depends directly on what has been our ability to save. This thought is very common worldwide. Whether you are a soccer player or not.

I will make a plea in favor of debt. When I say that people associate retirement with savings capacity, what we are really talking about is about equity. Savings are equity. Pure equity. The problem with equity is that it is what it is. There is no more. And people start cold sweating for this reason. Isn't true?

I will oppose debt and equity. Keep reading and you'll see why.

I've talked about financial freedom, passive income, about what is an asset or a liability, cash-flow, etc. As a players' advisor you have to be smart financially speaking. If you're not and you don't behave like that, how you pretend someone else to rely on you?

As I said, a good financial planning during a soccer player career consists on understanding that a player who wins a lot of money should spend the money he has earned investing in assets that generate recurring and infinite passive cash-flows. Once the flow is generated we can afford the luxury, as they say. It's not a matter of having income. The key is knowing where the money comes from and for how long the money will be coming in! That's the key. I hope you understand me gradually.

If you spend your salaries money on luxuries, your luxuries will last the same as your salaries. However, if the money you spend on luxuries comes from a passive cash-flow, you can hold the same luxury as long as the source of the income that pays it. That is, indefinitely. Did you understand how it goes?

And why do I speak about debt vs. equity? Because if it has been done as I have explained, and if, for example, the player and yourself have invested in real estate to rent which provide you a number of passive cash-flows which are not time-bound, you're not going to have any problem to have credit. That is, you not depend only on equity, savings, because you generate passive income, and also you will go to the bank and they will be happy to lend you money ... because you have assets! That's what I call acquiring good debt.

Someone may ask himself, why do I have to acquire debt? Because there is good debt and bad debt. Everything depends on the financial education each one of us have. **Bad debt is the one you pay, and good debt is one that others pay for you**. See? As a player, you start with an important salary, you use the money to buy assets that will generate you passive cash-flows, you spend some of the money of those flows on whatever you want and the rest you invest it again in other assets that generate more flow. When the player retires his cash-flow will be assured indefinitely because of having collected assets. Assets that, on the other hand, will give absolute trust to your bank to lend you more money to invest it in more assets that will generate new positive cash-flows, ie, it gives you an excess after deducting the expenses associated with the money acquisition. And so on and so forth. Wait because there's more.

So why just save? Why retire with your own money when you can retire with others money acquiring good debt? Take advantage of leverage, that is, the ability to do more with less. Savings have a deadline and don't give so much certainty to banks. I hope I was clear on this point. So, if once you are retired banks keep lending you money will mean that you've done things right. And if you acquire debt, make sure it is "good debt".

As a great agent you are practice what you preach. Do not give easy advice. People will believe what they see in you, not what you tell them.

PART III. WHAT A SOCCER AGENT SHOULD KNOW

What a players' agent can't be is ignorant. I really ask you to please don't be it. Many people are attracted to this business only for what they believe is going to be easy money. They can't be more wrong. The multidisciplinary education has to be as wide as possible, whether after you're going to delegate in people who are more specialized than you in the different fields. It is important for you to get this.

You must know, educate yourself constantly, and be up to date. Your clients trust you and you can't disappoint them. You must know the different variations that can occur and know how to manage them. Do not to forget that all the eyes will turn to you when bad things happen. It's like you were Mary Poppins bag. Do you remember the movie? Instead of removing items from the bag infinitely, you will need to have solutions with the same fluidity with which Mary Poppins removed gadgets from her travel bag. If you do so you will be a "supercalifragilisticexpialidocious" agent. You can be sure.

You have to specialize yourself, yes. But you have to do it in the activity you are going to perform. In your potential client. That is, soccer players' agent. It is very common to find a crowd of people who are officially soccer players' agents who are not focused on this activity. However, within the activity, within this specialization you must have an education base as wide as possible. Multidisciplinary in terms of "economic-legal-soccer".

It is true, that the beginning is not easy (what can I say that you don't know), but that complicated beginning will last, or even worse, not come to an end if you don't focus on this activity. Being an agent is not only about going to see a number of games in your free time, about seeing good players and talk to them or their parents. There is something like that, but that's not enough. **If you really want to be an agent, commit yourself. Be mentally prepared that this job is a long distance race. Of resistance**. You have to be aware of it. The contrary would be fooling yourself.

What can't be is that you want to be agent in case of. One is dedicated to his duties and then dedicates himself to "interfere" to see if he is lucky and he gets something. That to me is not worthy and generates job bad reputation. Figuratively, it is as if in a water transfer from one point to another there were a number of people in the middle waiting to pick up the water drops which could go falling. Being a good agent means being an active part in the transfer creation. And not only the creation, but also be a reference to say from where to where should go this transfer. Do you understand where I'm going?

1. <u>DISCRETION</u>

"Have more than you show; talk less than what you know". William Shakespeare

Be reasonable. Apply common sense. Caution and discretion are of the greatest intangible assets that you can have as an agent.

Many novice agents make public and proclaim everything that is going on. Why they do that? For an explosive mixture of ego and lack of self-confidence. Self-esteem is ego's jailer. Self-esteem knows when to let ego go out and when not. Without self-esteem ego is free will. In addition, ego, as good narcissist, likes the rest to see him. Stay afloat. And when he does it he uses imprudence and indiscretion.

When I see an agent that without being prompted, that is, on his own initiative, does nothing but talk about his virtues and capacities, of great operations and very good contacts, I do more than repeat myself the words of the Englishman historian Thomas Carlyle: *"Who can't keep his thoughts to himself, will be unable to do great things".*

And that *"discretion in words worth more than eloquence"* (Francis Bacon). Big agents as you should know and implement that. So have self-esteem and put it to work. Activate your particular inner "Jiminy Cricket" in order to be your alarm whenever the ego wants to emerge.

76

Discretion and prudence are upward values. Characteristics of capable, educated and high-mindedness people. Practice discretion. You won't regret it.

2. <u>THE AGENT AND THE SOCCER PLAYER EDUCATIONAL TRAINING</u>

Do not make your clients absolutely dependent people. In my case, one of my main interests is to let my clients see that despite having my help and advice, they shouldn't walk away from their stuff.

They shouldn't neglect anything concerning them. Including their business. That doesn't mean they have to be in that directly. It means that, despite not doing things by themselves, they need to be aware of the reasons why things are like they are. They should know their financial position at all times. And for that it is recommended that, as long as they are able to do so, they should learn and educate themselves on issues that affect them most directly. It's great to delegate, but to delegate you have to know things well enough to know what to delegate and how to do it.

Your clients need to have criteria. The present and future of your client can't be at the discretion of someone that chooses for him. They must have the intellectual ability to have a say in their spheres of competence. If not, they will be perpetually doomed to not being in control. Nothing will depend on them. Simply because they don't understand anything that is not strictly their profession. And that's not good.

The confidence that you place in other person has to be based on your own criterion. If not, the trust you have in someone will be determined by what others have said you have to do. And such situation is very good for those who have information and knowledge, as well as not very good intentions.

Beware, therefore, of your own and your clients ignorance. Make them people with concerns. Although it is only regarding their interests. It is not an easy task, but not trying would fall within what might be called professional irresponsibility. One way to deal with the issue would be capturing their attention and showing the benefits of being aware of everything concerning them and the learning that requires. Otherwise we could always refer to the possibility of loss. Issue that, no doubt about it, will capture their interest. Interest is the second step, after attention, which is required when being persuasive.

PART IV. CONCLUSIONS

As you may come to realize throughout this book I have tried to stay away from what would be a usual book on players' agents. I don't know if I've succeeded. If you've come this far I thank you.

I didn't want to write about a series of regulations and objective questions. I wasn't looking for that because, if you are interested, there are multiple books and documents easily accessible.

With this book I wanted to step on the mud. Give you my particular version of what happens in the profession everyday. Tell you which are the critical elements, because of their importance, you should pay special attention to. I was interested in telling you what this profession is about beyond the formalities. The formalities are that, formalities. I have tried to add my two cents. Make you part, from my experience, of what I understand are the minimum capabilities that anyone who is interested in developing this profession should have.

There are technical issues and regulations as well, but it was not my interest here to treat them. They don't provide the slightest added value. They are what they are. In my case, instead, I have tried to contribute with something with value. My personal experience. I hope I have contributed. I am satisfied if you have been able to collect some issues that you could consider helpful.

Twitter: @PaulFraga

www.futbolydineroresponsable.com

Printed in Great Britain
by Amazon